10 Steps To starting Up An Online Business

Giovanni Dangel

© **Copyright 2016 by Giovanni Dangel - All rights reserved.**

This document is geared towards providing exact and reliable information in regards to the topic and issue covered. The publication is sold with the idea that the publisher is not required to render accounting, officially permitted, or otherwise, qualified services. If advice is necessary, legal or professional, a practiced individual in the profession should be ordered.

- From a Declaration of Principles which was accepted and approved equally by a Committee of the American Bar Association and a Committee of Publishers and Associations.

In no way is it legal to reproduce, duplicate, or transmit any part of this document in either electronic means or in printed format. Recording of this publication is strictly prohibited and any storage of this document is not allowed unless with written permission from the publisher. All rights reserved.

The information provided herein is stated to be truthful and consistent, in that any liability, in terms of inattention or otherwise, by any usage or abuse of any policies, processes, or directions contained within is the solitary and utter responsibility of the recipient reader. Under no circumstances will any legal responsibility or blame be held against the publisher for any reparation, damages, or monetary loss due to the information herein, either directly or indirectly.

Respective authors own all copyrights not held by the publisher.

The information herein is offered for informational purposes solely, and is universal as so. The presentation of the information is without contract or any type of guarantee assurance.

The trademarks that are used are without any consent, and the publication of the trademark is without permission or backing by the trademark owner. All trademarks and brands within this book are for clarifying purposes only and are the owned by the owners themselves, not affiliated with this document.

Table of Contents

Introduction 1
Step 1 What You Will Be Selling 3
Step 2 Taking the First Steps 9
Step 3 Finding the Right Platform 15
Step 4 Finding an Online Payment Solution 21
Step 5 Catching and customer friendly site 27
Step 6 Include user reviews 33
Step 7 Create a Unique Logo 34
Step 8 Dealing with Customers 40
Step 9 Traffic Generation 46
Step 10 Stop, Reddit: 50
Conclusion 53

Introduction

I want to thank you and congratulate you for downloading the book, 10 steps to starting Up An Online Business.

This Book contain proven steps and strategies on How to start up online Business.

The following chapters will discuss the ways to help you achieve your online income dreams when it comes to finding the right type of product to sell, setting up your website, building your brand, driving traffic to your future site and more. The most important thing to remember is that it will take time to make your online dreams a reality, slow and steady wins the race. $

These days it seems like everyone is buying everything from electronics to food online and more and more online stores are popping up each day to take advantage of the ravenous demand. While it is great to know that the customers are out there, the competition is out in full force as well. This means that not only do you need to have a clear idea of what you want to sell, you need to have an even clearer idea of what you are going to do to set yourself apart from everyone else selling the same thing.

Thanks again for downloading this book, I hope you enjoy it!

Are you ready to transform your life and reach your optimal potential?

VISIT:

WWW.THEGENIUSPOWER.COM

Step 1
What You Will Be Selling

After you have decided to take the plunge and start an online business, the next thing you will need to do is determine what it is you are interested in selling. This is perhaps the most important decision you will make throughout the entire process as it will affect everything from what your website will look like to the places you can look when it comes to sourcing items successfully. In general, you will want to find a niche of individuals to serve that is small enough to not be overly crowded with vendors while at the same time being broad enough that people will find your store if they do a general Google search vaguely surrounding your topic. Finding the right niche will require some thought and you might find it helpful to start with the following.

Think of a Problem: The first thing you should consider when it comes to assessing the demand that a particular group of customers might have is how well they are currently served in the traditional online infrastructure. The best place to start when it comes to doing niche related research is with the communities that you yourself are a part of. From there, it is only a matter of asking yourself what problems you face on a regular basis and what items could successfully fulfil that need. Of special interest should be items that you purchase on the regular that are either difficult to procure easily or that you have to buy in bulk on a semi regular basis. Right down your list of ideas as they come to you so you don't miss out on any potential winners.

Determine the need: After you have generated a starting list you will now need to determine how in demand the items you thought of actually are. While it might seem difficult to get into the psyche of the consumer, in reality it has never been easier. To get started all you need to do is type a related word or phrase into Google or Bing and see what the auto fill options look like. What you should be hoping to find are indications that a type of demand is currently going unfulfilled which means queries like searches to find specific types of items are the ideal target. Depending on the types of results you find on Google, you may find it worthwhile to perform similar searches on eBay and Etsy.

Consider the existing market: After you have a good idea of the market that you are thinking about breaking into, the next thing you will want to do is find out what the general competition is going to be like in your new prospective market. While this won't allow you to see the types of margins they are working with, this should provide you with a way to get a feel for how active the customer market seems to be. While the market could be underserved, the alternative is that there isn't enough of a need to support a vibrant market, which is why this step is so important to your long term financial success.

Ideally you will want to Google search terms that might relate to your potential future niche and then check the websites that come up on the first page of Google. While there you will want to look at the quality of the available stock and pay special attention to the number of items that are currently exhibiting out of stock or low stock indicators. Additionally, you should see what customers are saying about the products and how many reviews they have received to give you an idea of how many customers they are working with.

It is equally important to be aware of the strength of the SEO of any major competitors that you identify in a given space. If you see the same handful of websites appear on the first page of the search results for several related searches around items that you might hope to sell, then you will need to figure out just how strong these companies SEO is if you hope to have a chance in the space. More than anything else, expert SEO on an established site can make it almost impossible for you to get the equivalent of random foot traffic to your fledgling store, clipping its wings before it has a chance to fly.

While looking into your possible future competitors and their affairs, it is important to keep an eye on each individual website for features and options that will make your own website more fully featured as well. Be sure to take note of the weaknesses as well as the strengths so you know where to improve upon implicitly. Additionally, you will want to consider the breadth of the product options available as well as the pricing, each one of these items is a potential area of competition if you try hard enough.

If you search turned up numerous options for purchasing the items in question, especially with little or no extra effort, then you will need to take a long hard look at the available products and determine what, if anything, you can do better. Unless the business seems brisk enough to warrant additional competition you better have a better spin or a cheaper supplier if you hope to shake up an existing and established marketplace. What's more, you will want to determine if the existing business are reputable and generally appreciated by customers, if this is not the case then you might be able to set yourself apart by simply offering quality customer service. If none of the above seems viable then you may want to consider another, less established niche instead.

Maintain perspective: If your first niche ends up looking as though it is already as crowded enough as it is, then it is important to not stay married to an idea that you have absolutely no investment in at this point. It is much better to find out that your first choice ended up not being as viable as you thought in the planning stage rather than when you have already made a significant investment into making your online store a reality. Maintain the right perspective and be ready to walk away up to the point that your website is live and ready to receive customers.

Consider the quality: When it comes to finding ways to set yourself apart from the competition, one of the best ways of doing so is by offering a better quality of product for relatively the same price. Depending on the types of items you are selling, being known for quality is more important than anything save an extreme price difference.

When given a choice the average consumer is likely to put quality first in terms of importance which is why you must ensure that whatever you end up selling you do whatever you need to in order to ensure that the quality of every product that your store sells be as high as possible. While it may be tempting to reduce your costs as thoroughly as possible early on, in reality this is less of an investment in the future and more of a guarantee that your first customers could be your only customers. A reputation for quality will spread quickly and can do more for a fledgling startup than just about any other marketing tool.

Step 2
Taking the First Steps

After you have a clear idea of what niche you are interested in targeting, as well as the general types of items you feel you might be able to find a demand for, the next thing you will need to do is figure out exactly what you will be selling and where it will be coming from. The specific types of sources that you will be able to use will vary dramatically depending on the niche and the type of products that you are looking for. Nevertheless, there are some things you need to decide before looking into vendors of all types that are universal and these are expounded upon below.

Consider where you want your items to come from: At this point, narrowing it down to overseas versus local vendors is enough. While products that are made overseas are often cheaper, they tend to also withstand less abuse before breaking. Likewise, certain items can be difficult to import based on various local restrictions. What's more, international mail can be more tumultuous than other types of shipping which can make it a nonstarter for products that are of a more delicate nature. Additionally, depending on the types of items you are selling, you can advertise that they are made in your country, which might be enough to set you apart from likeminded competitors.

Consider drop shipping: Depending on the market you are interested in breaking into, you may not actually need vendors of your own at all and could instead simply focus on getting orders and taking care of customers. If this sounds like a process you are interested in, then drop shipping might be for you. Drop shipping is a type of order fulfillment whereby the merchant, you, purchases items from a third party vendor after the item has already been purchased from you by a customer and the vendor then ships the item directly to the customer.

While this also means that you won't have to worry about storage fees, it mostly means that you will need to ensure you vendor is extremely reliable otherwise you could end up with angry customers and no way to pacify them. Your choice of vendors is also likely going to be much more limited, both to those who accept drop shipping agreements as well as to those in your own company as the international drop shipping market is largely nonexistent in many instances.

Additionally, dealing with returns when it comes to drop shipping company errors can be difficult because it is likely that neither you nor your customers will have a clear idea of who to speak with in order to ensure that the situation has been resolved. While drop shipping means that you don't have to put any money down on actual inventory, it also means you won't receive nearly as much of the profits as the drop shipping company will take a healthy percentage of every sale.

Consider Fulfilment by Amazon: If you are interested in working with an extremely reliable partner in a situation that is similar to drop shipping then you may want to look more thoroughly into the Fulfilment by Amazon Program. As an Amazon Affiliate you would find items that you think you will be able to sell for a tidy profit and ship them to Amazon who then takes care of the storage and shipping of the items in question after you post them to your Amazon store.

The items that you post are then eligible for free 2-day shipping while also being placed higher in the search results because of your relationship with Amazon. Additionally, you will be able to post links to your items as well as links to Amazon on your own website, doubling your online real estate. Like with drop shipping, the biggest downside here is that you will have to pay Amazon a percentage of each sale, a small monthly fee and storage fees related to the items that you are selling on their site.

Consider traditional vendors: If you feel as though you aren't sure where to start when it comes to finding a vendor that fits your needs, perhaps the best place to start is at a local trade show. While not traditionally advertised unless you are looking for them, wholesaler tradeshows are the perfect way for a new online merchant to talk to vendors in person, all of whom are anxious to give out the best deals possible in order to justify the cost of the booth they rented and the time they are spending standing on the show floor. This is great for you as it means everyone is eager to lower their prices and start profitable long term relationships. In fact, many of the only vendors that you may have been looking at actually get their products from similar shows and then sell them for a markup.

Overseas vendors: When it comes to finding the best prices on goods of all types, the cheapest options are always going to be distributors from Asia as long as you are willing to buy in bulk. As a new online merchant, there are several issues that will need to be overcome in order to complete this transaction successfully, the first of which is determining any international customs issues that you made need to overcome. If it looks like it may be difficult, or even just a mild struggle to get items through customs, consider how much of a hassle it will seem the fiftieth time you have to do it and then find a more efficient option.

The next thing you will want to keep in mind is the language barrier which can most likely be more easily mitigated by detailing specifics via email as opposed to over the telephone. While the people you are dealing with are likely comfortable speaking English, they are likely to read it even more comfortably which will lead to fewer surprises down the line. Along these same lines, it is especially important to read every draft of every contract extremely thoroughly as the rules of conduct regarding business contracts are often different in these circumstances which means the fifth draft of a contract could contain completely different specifics than the previous incarnations.

When creating a contract, it is especially important to indicate a clear and definite time table as to when the items will be successfully produced as well as shipped. This will ensure that your items are not waylaid unnecessarily, though it will not ensure that the quality is where it needs to be when you receive your first shipment. Besides the agreed upon timeframe, you will likely want to include enough time to receive 3 shipments before you can expect the quality you are comfortable selling to customers.

Once you have worked through all of the specific details and actually found a vendor that you think you can successfully work with, the most important thing you can do is ensure that this relationship remains open and mutually beneficial for years to come. This means staying in touch with your point of contact, both via email and the occasional phone call. Putting in the extra effort to create a real connection will help the vendor to see you as more than a name on a list and ensure they are more likely to take care of you when it matters most.

Step 3
Finding the Right Platform

Once you have found your niche and a vendor or two that will let you take advantage of it, the most important decision left to make is which type of commerce platform you want to use to sell your wares successfully. The commerce platform that you chose should be a reflection of the market you are working in as, if you choose properly, this platform could account for more than 75 percent of all of your business. Likewise, if you make the wrong choice, your online store will be dead in the water before it even gets going. Consider the following suggestions when it comes to selecting a partner and you'll be on your way to finding the right choice for you in no time flat.

Decide if you want to build your own site: Prior to getting online and sussing out your options, you will want to assess a few fundamentals to ensure you are moving forward in a way that is productive in the long term. The first decision you will want to make is if you want to design your own website to host your store or if you are fine with simply having a store page on an existing platform. If you go the platform route the costs will be much lower, but you won't have as much control over certain things like the presentation of your items or access to customer details.

Alternately, if you take the time to either pay for or build your own site you will still want to be affiliated with a platform but your site can be tweaked in such a way that it meets your specifications exactly. Along with this freedom comes additional responsibility, however, as you will need to do much more in terms of marketing to ensure that the investment in a unique website sees a return in the long run. Eventually, if marketed correctly, then the sales from your own site, of which no one else will take a cut, will outpace the platform sales which is when the extra effort you put in to creating a website will pay off.

Additional build your own website considerations: If you choose to create your own website from scratch, you will also need to consider what company you wish to host your site and how you want to handle point of sale transactions. When it comes to hosting your own website, the right choice for nearly everyone is to pay someone else to handle their hosting responsibilities and bite the bullet and pay the PayPal fees required to use their service to process payments. On the other hand, those who are already familiar with the requirements of coding a site from scratch can take that route, though if you aren't already proficient, this is like not the best way to learn.

Additional platform considerations: If you are instead more interested in signing up to sell things via a platform such as Etsy, Amazon or eBay, the amount of setup you will be required to commit to early on will be much more manageable. Additionally, the importance of additional advertising is somewhat lessened as the platform likely already gets a substantial amount of traffic each day.

If you take this path, then the most important things you will need to worry about is uploading your stock and ensuring the pictures are of the best quality possible. While this option is easier, it is also going to result in a lower level of overall profit in the long term as the platform that you choose to work on will take a percentage of each sale you make through their site. As previously mentioned, the best option is likely to do both so you can use the platform to develop a client base and then move them to your own site over time.

Ask yourself what is most important: To find the right platform to ensure your product receives the respect and sales it deserves; you will want to start by determining just what you want out of an ecommerce platform. If you aren't sure what, if any, special needs your product has then Shopify or even Amazon might be the best place to start. On the contrary, if you are working with a digital product, the most popular option in that space is currently Gumroad; while those interested in making money from a blog should look into Seiz. NuOrdr is the order of the day for business to business transactions and Celery is where those who are selling made-to-order products are currently seeing the most results.

The most important thing to remember when it comes to choosing the ecommerce platform that is right for you is that you should consider plenty of options and compare features and costs extensively prior to making any commitments. One especially important feature is the ability to personalize your page in ways that will set you apart from other sellers. The platform marketplace is crowded which means that you need to seize every possible opportunity when it comes to setting yourself apart from the crowd. Another important consideration is payment options as the more ways of users have of financially interacting with a given site, the better.

Don't forget about the backend: While having a pleasing frontend experience for users is an extremely important part of an ideal platform, it is only half of what matters to you as the proprietor of an only store. What this means for you is that you should take the time to ensure the platform you are eying offers plenty of options to make your life easier as well including things like quality customer service, accounting, analytics, sales reports, simple managing of orders, mobile inventory management, fulfillment, marketing, shipping and sales options. Additionally, it is important to keep in mind that many of your potential customers will be accessing this content via a smartphone or tablet which means that you will also need to consider the mobile platform offerings as well.

Further considerations if you are building your own site: If you are more interested in building your own website, they you still will be able to choose from multiple tiers of DIY. If you don't have the inclination or time to code your won site from the ground up, you will want to consider the myriad of self-hosted platforms that are currently offering their services. In these instances, you would essentially rent the space for your website from a company before doing all the extra work to create a functioning website from there.

If you are considering hosting your own site, it is crucial that you keep in mind the laws in your area regarding how online stores must process debit or credit card information. Additionally, you will need to keep in mind the various steps you will need to take in order to ensure that the information is secure via the rules outlined by governing body for such things which is known as the Payment Card Industry or PCI. In addition to following the rules and keeping your customers secure, as a new business owner you have an additional stake in keeping your customer's information safe as if they find out that you are the reason they had to get a new card, they will never be back to generate repeat business.

Step 4
Finding an Online Payment Solution

After you have decided on how to best go about choosing the platform that is right for you and your soon-to-be online store, the last step before actually creating your site is determining what types of payments you are going to accept. Assuming you have chosen a robust marketplace platform, then this may have already been taken care of for you and all you will need to do is connect a few dots to get things properly up and running. Even still, there are a few online payment considerations that need to be made to ensure that when you finally open your online store everything runs as smoothly as possible.

Find the right gateway for you: As a general rule, your online store will be expected to accept debit cards as well as credit cards, you may also accept checks or even wire transfers if you are so inclined though the cost benefit analysis of this process is mediocre at best. Finding the right gateway to asset you in this task is an important part of setting up an efficient online business. A payment gateway is one of any number of third party business that jointly verify credit or debit card information and process these payments so you do not need to do so by hand.

There are numerous payment gateway options to choose from, which means that finding the right one for you may be difficult. Nevertheless, it is important to persevere as choosing the right gateway is akin to choosing the right bank for your own finances. When first starting out, it is important to consider the various limitations on access that may occur, if a merchant account is required and the various costs associated with the service.

Of all of the payment gateway variables, the amount that each gateway charges for their services can vary the most dramatically depending on the level of service requires. When you are first starting out you will likely be able to subsist on a free PayPal account which will allow you to process a small number of transactions each month free of charge. PayPal then offers a professional account for a monthly fee. Additional payment gateway payment arrangements include a flat rate that is applied to each transaction (ideal for high-priced sales) or a percentage of each sale (great for low cost, repeat transactions). It is important to pick a gateway that is reliable and also one whose fee schedule fits your future-business plan.

Decide if you need a merchant account: When looking into payment gateways, it is important to ensure that you are aware which of the gateways you are considering requires users to have a merchant account before they can sign up. This is also a requirement for some ecommerce platforms so it is a good idea to know if you are going to need one at that point as well. If you are interested in getting your online store up and running as quickly as possible, as cheaply as possible, then you will most likely want to avoid this step if possible as it can often be difficult and has the possibility to be expensive as well.

Obtaining a merchant account: If you determine that you need a merchant account, be aware that the process is cumbersome and full of requirements. This is because it is created by the credit card companies as online merchants that are not up to snuff will only cause them countless headaches down the line. This can occur if a customer wants a refund that the merchant can't provide or if the merchant fails to deliver on the promised goods without returning the funds. The cost to process all of these transactions is also a factor which the credit card companies are anxious to pass on to merchants as well.

This starts as soon as you begin applying for a merchant account as it requires an application fee that is nonrefundable if you are rejected. Before you go ahead and pay the fee it is important to speak with a representative from the verification service that can explain exactly what they are looking for in qualified applicants and how long the approval process is going to take. While these pieces of information seem basic, nailing down specifics will be difficult, but it is important to keep at it to avoid wasting time as well as money. Be aware, getting a letter of approval or rejection can take as long as 3 months.

Surprisingly, gaining a merchant account can actually be easier for new businesses then established businesses who are looking to try a new form of payment as the fewer the number of transactions that are made per month, the less your store is costing the credit card companies. This is only true if you let the companies know you are a startup, however, as otherwise you may just look like an unprofitable business that isn't worth their time.

This means you will need to include a cover letter with your application explaining that you are a new business and what it is you are hoping to sell. Your letter should also include a description of any issues regarding eligibility that your account might face and how you will mitigate any concerns these issues might cause. This doesn't mean you will always succeed, however, but it certainly couldn't hurt. Alternately, if you have an online business that is already flourishing then you will want to include all of your financials as well as a lengthy list of transactions that you have already completed successfully.

Consider all of PayPal's options: If you aren't going to use an ecommerce platform right off of the bat, you will most likely want to consider PayPal as the easiest way to start accepting online payments as quickly as possible. After you have signed up for a merchant account, you will be able to add both shopping cart and buy now buttons to your site in a way that is both quick and easy. You will even be able to set up reoccurring orders or other types of subscriptions. Perhaps the best part is that PayPal is in charge of securing all of the important and relative data which means you don't need to worry about it in the slightest.

Creating a PayPal merchant account is as easy as entering relevant information and agreeing to their related terms. The information you entered will then be verified and you will immediately be able to use the service to begin receiving payments. You will also be allowed to modify relevant controls including if you wish to sell products to those who cannot verify an address, those who use different currencies or those who are living in another country. You can even determine what comes up on the related billing statement that is generated for the charge.

While adding the relevant checkout and shopping cart buttons to your site can be accomplished free of charge, once you begin seeing results from your hard work and customers begin actually buying things then you will be charged $0.30 per transaction, as well as 2.9 percent of each sale to start, with that dropping to 1.9 percent for those who do a steady amount of transactions. While there are certainly cheaper options available, none are as easy to set up and as widely trusted as PayPal.

Step 5
Catching and customer friendly site

Once you have worked out all of the other specifics, it is finally time to plan out just what your sit is going to look like. It is important that your site is as eye catching and customer friendly as possible, you only have a single chance to make the right first impression. Don't forget, confident design is good design which means that if your customers feel you are confident in your product, they are more likely to follow through with a purchase as well as come back and do it again.

Be aware of core design principles: The first of these is contrast as when used properly, contrast will make your online store look sharp and crisp while also making it look more organized without requiring you to change anything else. The best way to ensure your site has the right amount of contrast is to focus on colors that are different from one another while still being complimentary. It is also important to vary sizes and shapes between groups for the most contrasting results.

It is also important to take the time to determine how users will most likely proceed through your site if you hope to ensure that this process is as simple and painless as it can be. This means that your various categories and pages should be separated cleanly and in a way that is immediately clear to those who are viewing your page for the first time. If you don't take the time to ensure you page is aligned properly then you may see plenty of page views but significantly fewer sales.

Along similar lines, it is important to ensure that you utilize repeating patterns and styles as you move between pages. While it is easy to go overboard, the right amount of repetition will make your store feel more cohesive which means it will be more likely that customers will come back a second time. Finally, it is important to keep a critical eye on how the information on your site is arranged to ensure related information can be found easily between topics. Remember, the easier it is for customers to find what they are looking for, the more likely they are to continue interacting with your site.

Do not underestimate images: Each item that you post to your store should include pictures of the item directly as it is shipped so customers understand what they are getting when they click the purchase button. However, the first picture that you should include for every item should be a high quality picture of that item in use as it would be in the real world. Not only will this force the customer to put themselves in the shoes of the person using the item, it is more likely to cause them to engage with the product more thoroughly which can ultimately lead to a higher percentage of sales.

Each picture that you connect to an item should be large enough that the item can be seen clearly while also being expandable incase the customer wants to see something more clearly. Each of your items should always be displayed in the same way in these pictures so as to create a cohesive feel. The background that you choose for non-action shots should be something that is a single color, preferably white, as anything else is going to naturally draw the eye away from the item.

It is also important to ensure your pictures are large enough to be seen clearly, while at the same time not being so large that it makes your site load slowly as this will just drive away traffic. A picture that takes a few extra seconds to load is appropriate, anything more is simply letting form supersede function to the detriment of overall sales.

Be professional: When it comes to designing your store you will want to choose both the right types of fonts as well as the right types of colors in order to convey an air of professionalism that will make customers feel they can trust you to carry out a transaction. When it comes to choosing appropriate fonts, you will want to stick with 3 visual similar but unique fonts total for use throughout your site. You will want to start with the perfect font for any headings that you use on all of the pages you create. Additionally, you will want a separate font for the standard body text of any pages and another for pullouts or side panels as needed. The various sizes for the 3 fonts should always be the same as well as anything else will give off the message that your site is not professional.

When it comes to choosing the colors that will adorn your site it is important to be just as cohesive and consistent as you are with the fonts. The colors that you choose for your site will become a distinct part of the brand you are building for yourself which means you should pick them carefully as they may be around for a long time. Ideally, you will want to go with colors that fit the tone and theme of your site while also appealing to your primary audience. Don't forget about matching the colors to those of your industry as your individual products may clash otherwise. What's more, certain colors have negative connotations in certain circles, think read in the financial industry for example, and you need to be familiar enough with your topic to avoid these pitfalls.

Placing Content: When it comes time to actually lay down the placement for the words that will fill the pages of your site there are a few things you should keep in mind. The first is that, because most people read left to right, the right side of the screen is generally considered to be the most effective place to put your best deals or most important information. Customer interaction with this space is thought to be about 40 percent more consistent, across all age groups and types of consumers. This also makes this area the best place to include the information that will make it clear why your product is superior to that of your competitors.

The first page you will want to create is what is commonly referred to as the landing page. This is the first page of your site that people will see which is why it is important to include on it the most important information about your site as well as your most recent deals to encourage them to continue exploring more thoroughly. The information on your landing page should keep things short and simple as you have as little as 5 seconds to catch a new customer's attention. This means including words like click here or learn more might seem cliché but they are actually effective at drawing a customer's attention and letting them know where they can head to next.

Step 6
Include user reviews

Regardless of whether you are creating your own site from scratch or working through an established ecommerce platform, it is important to always provide your customers with a way to leave feedback about their products and experiences for other customers to view. Not only will this make it easier for you to track the satisfaction that your customers feel in regards to your products and services, but customer reviews are one of the most frequently cited examples of why a customer purchased a product. Do yourself a favor and ensure your customers can tell everyone how great your products are.

Step 7
Create a Unique Logo

The final thing you will need to decide on for your online store is a logo which will quickly and accurately summarize everything that's unique about your store in a single image. Needless to say, it is rather important but luckily you have already laid most of the groundwork when it comes to determining the right logo for your business. You already know what colors your brand uses, what is unique about your products as well as your store specifically as well as an overall feel for the tone your store will be trying to capture, all you have to do is put them together in the right way.

The importance of the logo when it comes to branding your product cannot be overstated. It is the part of your brand that is going to be seen on every email, every page of your site and on every advertisement that you ultimately pay for. This means there are a number of considerations you should keep in mind whether you are creating your own logo or just putting together ideas to explain to a professional what you are looking for. A good logo is well thought out and reiterated upon numerous times until it is absolutely perfect. Take the time to put together the best logo possible and the results you see because of it will increase significantly.

Elements of a good logo: The best logos are those that can be instantly associated with a specific company as well as what that company represents in terms of both culture and values. If used correctly your logo can concisely express the ideals and goals of your online store with a single glance, explaining the ideals behind your brand without a conscious thought. Likewise, you will want your logo to be memorable which means that repetition is going to be key to its efficacy in terms of long term recognition.

As such, incorporating a common symbol into your logo is a great way to jumpstart that recognition as when done properly it allows the business in question to hijack any other instances of that symbol for the purpose of improving brand awareness. Your logo should also be bold and vibrant enough to catch the eye of the average passerby and clear enough that its message can be absorbed in an instant. When used properly, a good logo is a seal of approval as well as a guarantee as to the quality of the products that are sold under it. Build a reputation as a fair purveyor of quality goods and others who value the same will seek out your logo and the promise that comes with it.

A good logo is versatile: When thinking about facets of your logo, it is important to prioritize versatility over specificity. It is important to keep in mind that the logo you are working to create will be used on numerous different items in numerous different shapes, sizes and colors. This means you need something easily recognizable regardless of all other variables, which can be easier said than done which is why it is important that you check your logo in numerous usage scenarios before adding it to your site.

This is why most photographs do not make good logos as they can only be manipulated to a certain point before they are no longer viable while also being rather limiting when it comes to color choice. The same goes for the font you chose for your company name as you don't want to go with anything that is extremely common or anything that is too garish or elaborate to be clearly understood, and don't forget, size is still a factor as well. You should always check your logo at the size of an average thumbnail, at a larger banner ad size and finally as a full screen sample, if it looks good across all three then you might have a winner on your hands.

Think about the emotion your logo evokes: While the colors of your site in general are a good jumping off point, it is of the upmost importance that your logo caters to an appropriate emotion related to the products you are hoping to sell. Studies have shown time and again that specific colors can lead to specific actions, up to and including making a customer more likely to follow through on a purchase. As such, the primary color of your logo, even if you come out with variations later on, can be thought of as a direct correlation to the voice of your store, though your logo should always look good in black and white, regardless, just in case.

Be aware of the long term potential for your logo: When designing your logo, it is important to try and find a style that feels timeless rather than cashing in on a trend that is popular in the short term. While playing off of something that is currently popular might seem like an easy solution right now, it will quickly become outdated and leave you in the same spot as before. Instead, try and stick with clean, simple logos that are more likely to stand the test of time. It is important to avoid switching logos frequently as there is no point to having a logo if no one can identify your online store by its appearance.

Use the right types of images: When it comes to the way your logo is formatted, you will want to avoid raster images at all times as they are made up of lots and lots of tiny pixel that become readily visible if the image is enlarged past a certain point. As such, .jpeg, .gif, .bmp and .psd file types should be avoided in favor of a vector image. Vector images make it easy to scale to practically any size, big or small, and while they can be more difficult to generate, they are unquestionably worth it.

When it comes to images it is also important to avoid the temptation to create something quick and easy with the help of stock images. Stock images negate the entire purpose of having a logo, however, as anyone can come along and create something extremely similar and there is little you can do to stop them. Stick with something completely original to maximize the potential of your logo's power.

Avoid clichés: While tapping into the collective unconscious to find themes and images that might work for your logo is a good place to start, sticking with the most obvious associations possible is only going to tell potential customers that you aren't terribly creative. What's worse, if you stick with the most common extrapolation of themes common to your niche then you run the risk of creating a logo that is extremely similar to the logo of other competitors in the market which will only lead to brand confusion in the long term? This is why it is important to work past the most obvious visual associations and find something that can be unique to your store and the brand you are creating.

Step 8
Dealing with Customers

After your site is fully set up and actually serving as a means for customers to purchase your inventory, there will be a number of things for you to keep in mind to ensure your customers are as happy as possible. Happy customers leave more positive item reviews and are more likely to become repeat customers as well. As long as you take the following suggestions into account, your customers should come away from every type of interaction extremely satisfied.

Start with the basic experience: The first thing you will want to keep in mind is how easy it is for customers to come to your store, find the items they are interested in and purchase them in a convenient and secure fashion. This process should be fluid, and error free, every time across all platforms which means quick load times and integrated touch controls for mobile access. The more varied and simple ways a customer can start buying things from you, the better.

Ensure your policies are simple: These days, customers are used to expecting arcane customer service policies regarding returns and sometimes even when it comes to basic things like shipping. This is an easy opportunity for you to set yourself apart by making the entire customer services experience as simple and easy to understand as you possibly can. This also goes for the types of products that you sell and all of the details you have on the product should be passed on to your customers as well.

If customers know exactly what to expect then they are less likely to need customer service in the first place. This means notifying customers of potential delays as soon as they become apparent as well as realistic expectations as to when the item will be back in stock and taking full responsibility for any delays. As long as you offer appropriate compensation for any difficulties, your customers won't remember any of the negative parts of the experience after it is all said and done, they will only remember how much you did to make things right.

Help customers find your products: Once customers have taken the time to come to your website, presumably in hopes of buying things, the least you can do is make it easy for them to find the products they are looking for. This means that you should have all of your items clearly broken down into appropriate categories while also offering detailed search functionality for those who know exactly what it is they are looking for. Each and every item that you are selling should be individually tagged with numerous keywords and your search function should also let individuals search based on various variables such as price or size if appropriate. While tagging each item uniquely will take some time, doing so will literally directly translate into additional sales month after month and year after year.

You will also want to include an FAQ section that includes all of the specific questions that you expect customers to have regarding the products you sell. This FAQ should include a hyperlinked table of contents to make it as easy for customers to find an answer to their questions as possible. A good place to start when it comes to your FAQ is things like store credit in regards to returns, overall return policy, any unique shipping concerns as well as information about you, your store and your products. The FAQ should also include a direct email link that allows customers to email you with unanswered questions directly. Emails that you receive to this email address should be replied to in a quick and courteous timeframe.

Always be professional: The best online businesses flourish because they don't use the fact that they are operating online as an excuse to be unprofessional. Likewise, it is important that you approach any interaction with customers with this in mind and strive to make every effort to provide the sort of customer service that you yourself would like to receive when it comes to dealing with an online store. Remember, you are now reliant on each and every person you interact with in this capacity to help you pay your bills day in and day out, act like it.

As a general rule, people will generally be contacting you in a customer service capacity in an effort to find someone to let them vent. Taking their initial dissatisfaction with a grain of salt and making it clear that their issue is actively being resolved is typically enough to make them change their tune significantly. Every opportunity to speak with a potential customer is extremely important to the long term success of your venture; treat them as such and you will find you suddenly have a steady supply of lifetime customers.

This also goes for negative reviews, seek out those who leave them and work with them to make the situation right in their eyes. Doing so can change negative reviews into those that are glowingly positive instead. Those who take the time to leave detailed negative reviews can also be those who speak out most loudly in your favor, you just need to give them the incentive and the opportunity to do so.

Always promise less than what you feel you can deliver: When it comes to making your customers happy, especially early on when you aren't quite sure if all of your ducks are really in a row, the best course of action is to always promise less than you feel relatively confident you can deliver. This means that if you think you can have an item delivered in 3 days' time, promise a 5-day delivery window, that way when the product shows up in just 3 days you exceeded customer expectations and if it takes a couple of extra days, that's fine too. It is always better to lower customer expectations early on, rather than having to rain on their parade later on.

Talk to your customers: As soon as your store is up and running, you should go ahead and create a mailing list as a way of opening up a dialogue between yourself and your customers. This will provide you with a way of directly interacting with the customers who like your product the most and its importance cannot be overstated. It is also important to send out customer surveys, especially early on, as a way of helping you determine what your customers like the most about your site and also the areas you can improve in. The people who like what you are selling enough to sign up to learn more about it are exactly the people you want to make as happy as possible, find out what they like and sell it to them. It really doesn't get any easier than that.

Be generous with rewards: People like getting things for free, that is a simple fact of life that you can easily use to your advantage. Consider including a small free gift with every purchase, or implementing some type of program where buying a certain number of items means the customer gets one free. It doesn't take much to keep customers coming back and a small investment in free gifts now can result in serious gains in the long term. No need to start with something extravagant, something useful in the $10 is enough to show your customers how much you care.

Step 9
Traffic Generation

After you finally have your entire online business up and running, as well as having the tools to help customers buy as much as possible in place, the last thing you will need to focus on is marketing your site to ensure your target audience is aware of your ability to service their needs. Initially this means ensuring your SEO is on point and keeping tabs on your Google search result rank, but it is also about much more than that. The primary battlefield of the online store is the first page of any search results, the most effective online merchants, and focus on additional advertising avenues to see the most effective results.

Understand your audience: As long as you are fully aware of your product and theoretically who may be ready to buy it, then you are already well on your way to understanding your audience. Likewise, sending out customer surveys is a great way to get the basics of the demographics that you are looking for. Once you have a general outline that represents your customer base the next step is to go deep and determine who their social media influencers are. These can be either

YouTube or other social media personalities who are extremely popular in certain demographics.

Once you understand who these people are, you will want to consume a fair bit of their content to get an idea of the types references they make and the types of slang they use. If you want your customers to connect with your brand you are going to want them to feel like they are embracing one of their own. Once you have appropriated the appropriate culture, the next step is to send your products directly to these influencers in hopes that they will like what you have sent and then ideally use or talk about it at some point down the line. While this might initially seem expensive, this should be considered a marketing expense and its results can be extremely lucrative.

It is important to not leave Instagram influencers out of the equation either as recent studies indicate that items that were positively rated by top influencers were directly correlated to an increase of sales of nearly 30 percent, what's more, nearly all of those customers were new to the site which means this type of exposure can be extremely influential. When it comes to creating a buzz around your brand, this type of marketing will give your store a grass roots feel that is extremely popular among the demographics that are the most likely to use the internet to buy goods and services on a regular basis. To find more information on popular influences, Websta.com can provide lists of the most commonly searched for usernames for Instagram and other sites, it also allows you to search hashtags.

Target traditional and video bloggers: There are countless popular traditional bloggers expressing their opinions to legions of loyal fans every day. You can interact with these individuals in multiple ways. The first is to treat them as you would any other influencer, or you could send out a press release type of document outlining why your store deserves to receive coverage. This option is utilized extensively which is why the first approach is likely going to be more successful unless there is something about your store that really sets it apart from the pack.

Additionally, there is a whole strata of individuals who exist as YouTube personalities solely thanks to their affinity for taking new items out of their boxes and talking about them for a little while. This is clearly a trend that you can take advantage of and as long as you can find a simple link to the types of products that the

YouTube personality works with and your products specifically, then send products out and send them out frequently. All told, your goal should be to get your products, and more importantly the name of your online store and your logo in front of as many pairs of eyes as possible.

Step 10
Stop, Reddit:

As far as creating a buzz around things that exist on the internet, one of the current leaders of the pack is Reddit.com. Practically any niche, including the one that your products are a part of, has its own r/ page and you should make a habit of hanging out in this space on a regular basis. If you have a product that you think will genuinely create a discussion then you can go ahead and post it, but you are better served in this instance by becoming a personality that the community recognizes and then linking to relevant items as they present themselves.

As long as you take a soft touch when it comes to selling, you can create a legion of loyal followers who don't even realize they are being marketed at. If this doesn't seem like something that would work for the products you have purchased, your next best bet is to look into advertising on these specific subreddits pages as you know that the people on those pages are going to be interested in your products by default. Having an ability to target an audience in this way can be extremely powerful and it is not an avenue that many people pursue.

Create associated content: If you are looking for additional ways to get people interested in visiting your website, you may want to consider giving them ancillary reasons for doing so. When you spent all that time researching products and your competitors, you likely gained quite a bit of knowledge about the related field, knowledge that other people who are interested in the products you are selling may be interested in as well. If you create content on a regular basis, then people will have a reason to visit your site and be more agreeable when you try to sell them things at the end of each post.

If you don't feel up to the challenge of creating your own content, your site could instead focus as an aggregation source for the type of content that you know your audience is interested in seeing. Additionally you can use other types of social media to include links to these articles as they are posted on your site which will help create a general awareness of your brand even if many of the potential customers might not be planning on buying anything right this minute.

Regardless of how you get them there, once you have new eyes on your website you will want to get them to stick around by asking them to sign up for your newsletter or by offering forums where people can discuss relevant topics. If you nurture the type of website that people want to interact with you will be able to generate a greater number of sales organically.

Conclusion

Thank for making it through to the end of this book, let's hope it was informative and was able to provide you with all of the tools you need to set up a successful online store. Once you have your store up and running it is important to not let the opportunity go to waste by losing steam in the maintenance phase.

Finally, if you enjoyed this book, then I'd like to ask you for a favor, would you be kind enough to leave a review for this book on Amazon? It'd be greatly appreciated!

Click here to leave a review for this book on Amazon!

Thank you and good luck!

www.ingramcontent.com/pod-product-compliance
Lightning Source LLC
Chambersburg PA
CBHW070333190526
45169CB00005B/1873